THE BRITTLE AGE *and*
RETURNING UPLAND

THE BRITTLE AGE *and*
RETURNING UPLAND

René Char

Translated by Gustaf Sobin

COUNTERPATH PRESS

DENVER

2009

Counterpath Press
Denver, Colorado
www.counterpathpress.org

L'Âge cassant and *Retour amont* are excerpted from *Oeuvres Completes* by René Char, © Editions Gallimard, Paris.

Thanks to Jennifer Pap for editorial guidance and assistance preparing this volume.

Printed in the United States of America

Library of Congress Cataloging-in-Publication Data

Char, René, 1907–1988.
[Âge cassant. English]
The brittle age, and, Returning upland / René Char ; translated by Gustaf Sobin.

    p. cm.
ISBN 978-1-933996-11-0 (pbk. : alk. paper)
I. Sobin, Gustaf. II. Char, René, 1907–1988. Retour amont. English. III. Title. IV. Title: Returning upland.
PQ2605.H3345A6513   2009
841'.912—dc22

                    2008053279

Distributed by Small Press Distribution (www.spdbooks.org)

Contents

Foreword: The Just Place

In the Vaucluse, where I've lived so many past summers in a simple field dwelling called a "Cabanon," there have been two poets of legend and true history. Petrarch, some time ago, and René Char, until his recent disappearance. For us, who reside there and live and love there, his spirit is, like Petrarch's, very much present, and the disappearance, only apparent. The same waters that nourished the Fontaine de Vaucluse, honored by the Italian poet, still flow into the language of Provence and its poetry as into the land—and all of that is the truth, even now, of the place.

My family and I moved to a hill town near René Char's L'Isle-sur-Sorgue to be near him. He came to our tiny stone house, called "le cabanon Biska" (for its former complaining inhabitants: "bisquer" in the local patois), loved our children, and welcomed them often in his home, called "Les Busclats," where he picked melons and potatoes with them, and gave them packets of marshmallows from the pharmacy. They called him "renéchar" and drew him pictures;

he kept their photographs in his glass-fronted bookcase. It was a simple relationship he had with all of us, as was ours with him and his poetry. The poetry was, after all, in the names of dwellings like ours and his, and places: le Mont Ventoux, le Thor, Sénanque, Gordes, Buis-les-Baronnies, Mérindol. We loved the places, the poems, and the poet.

Among the translators of this so beloved poetry was Gustaf Sobin, who was my friend and a superb writer and ethnographer. Gustaf is the one who rescued my Citroën 2CV when it refused to go up the hill, where we were joining Char's great friend and ours Tina Jolas, in a tiny village near Mérindol. He coaxed the dilapidated car into motion, and we went up all three: Gustaf, the 2CV, and myself. That was upland in another sense, but not a trivial one.

Gustaf Sobin has seized the spirit of this poetry and this poet with impeccable discretion and what seems to me an unwavering sense of justice to the text. In the case of René Char, this goes past the ordinary fidelity we translators owe to any author we deal with—in this case, something else is required. If I use the word "justice," I am of course thinking of "le mot juste," but also of a fairness demanded by the land and the very air. So, not just "faithful" but "fair." Gustaf's renderings are all that, and deserve their salute, still upland.

MARY ANN CAWS

Translator's Preface

One can grow more in the light of another person's expectations, occasionally, than in that of one's own. I remember growing, assimilating, refining my own sensibilities, within the gaze—complicitous as it was paternal—of the poet René Char. He'd taken me under wing from my first months in Provence, and endowed me (as he would other people, other things) with exaggerated qualities. Massive in stature, he himself magnified, aggrandized, blew into luminous proportions, whatever his attention happened to light upon. And it lit, indeed, upon virtually everything. A butterfly might announce a thunderstorm just as much as a breeze, the body of his beloved. His universe was inductive, driven—alchemically—by an irrepressible will toward the transformed.

Arriving as I did from North America as a young man (I was twenty-seven in 1963), I had everything to learn. And learn I did. René Char taught me, first, to read particulars: that the meticulously observed detail, drawn from nature, could provide the key to the deepest reaches of the imaginary. One and the other, the visible and the invisible, were but the interface of a single, singular, vibratory surface: that of the poem itself. The poem as response, as vector, as the vehicle of an irreversible human affirmation: here, indeed, was heady stuff for a young American, emerging out of a society (and thus a linguistics) dominated by the monophonics of the individual self.

The verb, suddenly, no longer reflected but expanded upon the given fields of experience. It offered alternatives. In scrupulously tracking the very trajectories of desire, it led one onto the sonorous landscapes of the revelatory.

For twenty-five years, this "Ligurian," as Picasso called him, this rural aristocrat, quixotic as lightning and ruminative as the braided river reeds in his beloved Sorgue, kept watch. He loaned me books, blankets, money whenever I needed it. More, far more, he taught me my trade. Had he, in fact, perceived in me something I hadn't? Some latent potential? Or had I simply grown within the magnifying ring of his hyperbole, attempting to match in words what his all too generous heart had projected into the depths of an all too grateful protégé?

GUSTAF SOBIN, 1988

L'ÂGE CASSANT /
THE BRITTLE AGE

To Docteur Jean-Louis Lévy,
in memory of his daughters,
Françoise and Madeleine

Je suis né comme le rocher, avec mes blessures. Sans guérir de ma jeunesse superstitieuse, à bout de fermeté limpide, j'entrai dans l'âge cassant.

I was born, like the rock, with my wounds. Uncured of my superstitious youth, my limpid firmness exhausted, I entered the brittle age.

En l'état présent du monde, nous étirons une bougie de sang intact au-dessus du réel et nous dormons hors du sommeil.

In the present state of the world we stretch, above reality, a candle of untainted blood, and we sleep outside of sleep.

Ce qui partout domine sans être aperçu: les alchimies et leurs furolles.

What rules everywhere without being noticed: the alchemies and their jack-o'-lanterns.

Le créateur est pessimiste, la création ambitieuse, donc optimiste. La rotation de la créature se conforme à leurs prescriptions adverses.

The creator is pessimist; the creation, ambitious and therefore, optimist. The creature's rotation conforms to their opposing prescriptions.

Dans la fidélité, nous apprenons à n'être jamais consolés.

In fidelity we learn never to be consoled.

Sans l'appui du rivage, ne pas se confier à la mer, mais au vent.

Without the support of the shore, don't confide in the sea but in the wind.

J'ai de naissance la respiration agressive.

I've had, since birth, an aggressive breathing.

Il faut saluer l'ombre aux yeux mi-clos. Elle quitte le verger sans y cueillir.

We should greet the shade with her half-closed eyes. She withdraws from the orchard without plucking.

Souffrir du mal d'intuition.

To suffer from the ache of intuition.

Sur la poésie la nuit accourt, l'éveil se brise, quand on s'exalte à l'exprimer. Quelle que soit la longuer de sa longe, la poésie se blesse à nous, et nous à ses fuyants.

Upon poetry night hastens, awakening breaks whenever we are enthused in expressing it. However long its tether, poetry wounds itself in our hands as we are wounded, in turn, by its escapings.

Il advient que notre coeur soit comme chassé de notre corps. Et notre corps est comme mort.

Sometimes our heart seems as if chased from our body, and our body, as if dead.

L'impossible, nous ne l'atteignons pas, mais il nous sert de lanterne. Nous éviterons l'abeille et le serpent, nous dédaignerons le venin et le miel.

We never attain the impossible, but it serves us as lantern. We will shun the bee and the snake, we will scorn the venom and the honey.

L'aubépine en fleurs fut mon premier alphabet.

The flowering hawthorn was my first alphabet.

Confort est crime, m'a dit la source en son rocher.

Comfort is crime, the fountain told me from its rock.

Sois consolé. En mourant, tu rends tout ce qui t'a été prêté, ton amour, tes amis. Jusqu'à ce froid vivant tant de fois recueilli.

Be consoled. In dying you return everything that you were lent, your love, your friends. Even that living coldness, harvested over and over.

La grande alliée de la mort, celle où elle dissimule le mieux ses moucherons: la mémoire. En même temps que persécutrice de notre odyssée, qui dure d'une veille au rose lendemain.

Death's great ally, where its midges are best concealed, is memory: the persecutor of our odyssey, lasting from an eve to the pink tomorrow.

L'homme: l'air qu'il respire, un jour l'aspire; la terre prend les restes.

Man: the air that he inhales one day inhales him; the earth takes the remainders.

O mots trop apathiques, ou si lâchement liés!
Osselets qui accourez dans la main du tricheur
bienséant, je vous dénonce.

O words, too apathetic or so loosely linked. Knuckle-bones, tumbling into the hand of the decorous trickster, I denounce you!

Tuer, m'a décuirassé pour toujours. Tu es ma décuirassée pour toujours. Lequel entendre?

To kill has unsteeled me forever.
You're my unsteeled one, forever.
Which should we read?

Qui oserait dire que ce que nous avons détruit valait cent fois mieux que ce que nous avions rêvé et transfiguré sans relâche en murmurant aux ruines?

Who would dare to say that what we have destroyed was worth a hundred times more than what we had dreamt and ceaselessly transfigured in murmuring to the ruins?

Nul homme, à moins d'être un mort-vivant, ne peut se sentir à l'ancre en cette vie.

No man, unless he be dead in living, can feel at anchor in this life.

L'histoire des hommes est la longue succession des synonymes d'un même vocable. Y contredire est un devoir.

The history of man is a long succession of synonyms for the same vocable. To contradict it is a duty.

Ce qui fut n'est plus. Ce qui n'est pas doit devenir. Du labyrinthe aux deux entrées jaillissent deux mains pleines d'ardeur. A défaut d'un esprit, qu'est-ce qui inspire la livide, l'atroce, ou la rougissante dispensatrice?

What was, no longer is. What isn't must become. Two hands, full of fervor, from the labyrinth with its twin openings, spring out. For want of a spirit, what instigates the livid, the atrocious, or the blushing dispensator?

Comment la fin justifierait-elle les moyens? Il n'y a pas de fin, seulement des moyens à perpétuité, toujours plus machinés.

How would the end justify the means? There is no end, only and forever the means, always more machinated.

Otez le souffle d'oeuvre, sa dynastie inconcevable; renvoyez les arts libéraux, qu'ils cessent de tout réfléchir, c'est le charnier.

Taking away the breath of work, its inconceivable dynasty, setting back the liberal arts until they no longer reflect on anything, this is the boneheap.

L'incalculable bassesse de l'homme *sous* l'homme, par fatalité et disposition, peut-elle être fondue par un coeur durable? Quelques-uns, indéfiniment, se glacent ou se dévastent sur ce chantier héréditaire.

Can the immeasurable baseness of man *under* man, through inclination and fatality, be dissolved by a steadfast heart? Some are indefinitely freezing or ruining themselves upon this hereditary worksite.

Quoi que j'esquisse et j'entreprenne, ce n'est pas de la mort limitrophe, ou d'une liberté hasardeuse et haussée qui s'y précipite, que je me sens solidaire, mais des moissons et des miroirs de notre monde brûlant.

In whatever I trace and undertake, I feel bound neither to a bordering death nor to its rush in a heightened and hazardous freedom, but to the mirrors and harvests of our burning world.

Il eut jusqu'au bout le génie de s'échapper; mais il s'échappa en souffrant.

He had, up to the last, a genius for escaping;
but he escaped, suffering.

Supprimer l'éloignement tue. Les dieux ne meurent que d'être parmi nous.

To abolish distance kills. The gods only die by being among us.

Lécher sa plaie. Le bal des démons s'ouvre au seul musicien.

Lick one's wound. Only the musician is admitted to the dance of the demons.

A la fois vivre, être trompé par la vie, vouloir mieux vivre et le pouvoir, est infernal.

At the same time living, being deceived by life, wishing to live and being able to live a better life, is infernal.

Il y avait dans cet homme toutes les impatiences et les grimaces de l'univers, et même exactement le contraire. Cela diminuait son amertume, donnait une saveur perfide à son espoir qui, ainsi aliéné, ne se dérobait pas.

This man had all the eagerness and grimaces of the universe as well as their exact opposites. It lessened his bitterness and gave an aspect of cunning to his hope which, being alienated, didn't give way.

Le malheur se récompense souvent d'une affliction plus grande.

Misfortune often rewards itself with a greater affliction.

"Je me révolte, donc je me ramifie." Ainsi devraient parler les hommes au bûcher qui élève leur rébellion.

"I revolt, therefore I ramify." This is how men should speak to the stake that raises their rebellion.

Quand le soleil commande, agir peu.

When the sun commands, move the least.

Comme la nature, lorsqu'elle procède à la réfection d'une montagne après nos dommages.

Like nature when it moves forth to remake, after our injuries, a mountain.

VENASQUE

Les gels en meute vous rassemblent,
Hommes plus ardents que buisson;
Les longs vents d'hiver vont vous pendre.
Le toit de pierre est l'échafaud
D'une église glacée debout.

VENASQUE

Gathered by the frost in droves,
Men more burning than the bush,
The long winds of winter will hang you.
The stone roof is the scaffold
Of a church that, upright, froze.

L'inclémence lointaine est filante et fixe. Telle, un regard fier la voit.

The distant inclemency, as seen by a noble gaze, is both flowing and fixed.

Si vous n'acceptez pas ce qu'on vous offre, vous serez un jour des mendiants. Mendiants pour des refus plus grands.

If you don't accept what is offered to you, one day you will be beggars: beggars to even greater refusals.

On ne découvre la vraie clarté qu'au bas de l'escalier, au souffle de la porte.

True clarity is only found at the base of the stairway, at the breath of the door.

Veuillez me vêtir de tendre neige, ô cieux, qui m'obligez à boire vos larmes.

Kindly clothe me in tender snow, O heaven that compels me to drink your tears.

La douleur est le dernier fruit, lui immortel, de la jeunesse.

Sorrow is the last fruit, itself immortal, of youth.

Se mettre en chemin sur ses deux pieds, et, jusqu'au soir, le presser, le reconnaître, le bien traiter ce chemin qui, en dépit de ses relais haineux, nous montre les fétus des souhaits exaucés et la terre croisée des oiseaux.

To set out on both feet and, until evening, to press, to recognize, to respect this road that shows us, despite its hateful relays, the straws of granted wishes and the earth, criss-crossed with birds.

RETOUR AMONT /
RETURNING UPLAND

This flight, wending toward the summit
(toward the very composition of knowledge,
dominant over empires) is only one of the
passages within the labyrinth. *But this*
passage that from lure to lure must be
followed in our quest for being *we can in no*
way avoid.

—Georges Bataille,
L'Expérience intérieure

I

Couchés en terre de douleur,
Mordus des grillons, des enfants,
Tombés de soleils vieillissants,
Doux fruits de la Brémonde.

Dans un bel arbre sans essaim,
Vous languissez de communion,
Vous éclatez de division,
Jeunesse, voyante nuée.

Ton naufrage n'a rien laissé
Qu'un gouvernail pour notre coeur,
Un rocher creux pour notre peur,
O Buoux, barque maltraitée!

Tels des mélèzes grandissants,
Au-dessus des conjurations,
Vous êtes le calque du vent,
Mes jours, muraille d'incendie.

C'était près. En pays heureux.
Élevant sa plainte au délice,
Je frottai le trait de ses hanches
Contre les ergots de tes branches,
Romarin, lande butinée.

I

Lying in a land of sorrow,
Bitten by crickets and children,
Fallen from obsolescent suns,
Sweet fruit of la Brémonde.

In a lovely, swarmless tree
You yearn for communion,
You shatter from division,
Youth, storm-cloud that sees.

Your shipwreck has left nothing
But a rudder for our heart,
A hollow rock for our fear,
O Buoux, mishandled boat!

Like larches that stretch,
Above conspiracies,
You are the tracing of the wind,
My days: a rampart of flame.

It was near. In a happy land.
Raising her complaint to delight
I rubbed the line of her hips
Against the spur of your branches,
Rosemary, heath the bee plunders.

De mon logis, pierre après pierre,
J'endure la démolition.
Seul sut l'exacte dimension
Le dévot, d'un soir, de la mort.

L'hiver se plaisait en Provence
Sous le regard gris des Vaudois;
Le bûcher a fondu la neige,
L'eau glissa bouillante au torrent.

Avec un astre de misère,
Le sang à sécher est trop lent.
Massif de mes deuils, tu gouvernes:
Je n'ai jamais rêvé de toi.

Stone after stone, I endure
My house's demolition.
Only the death-devoted, one evening,
Knew the exact dimension.

Winter was thriving in Provence
Under the gray gaze of the Vaudois.
The pyre melted the snow,
The water slid scalding in the torrent.

With a star of affliction
Blood is too slow in drying.
Range of my mournings, you rule:
I have never dreamt about you.

II

Traversée

Sur la route qui plonge au loin
Ne s'élève plus un cheval.
La ravinée dépite un couple;
Puis l'herbe, d'une basse branche,
Se donne un toit, et le lui tend.
Sous la fleur rose des bruyères
Ne sanglote pas le chagrin.
Buses, milans, martres, ratiers,
Et les funèbres farandoles,
Se tiennent aux endroits sauvages.
Le seigle trace la frontière
Entre la fougère et l'appel.
Lâcher un passé négligeable.
Que faut-il,
La barre du printemps au front,
Pour que le nuage s'endorme
Sans rouler au bord de nos yeux?
Que manque-t-il,
Bonheur d'être et galop éteint,
Hache enfoncée entre les deux?
Bats-toi, souffrant! Va-t'en, captif!
La transpiration des bouchers
Hypnotise encore Mérindol.

Crossing

On the path that plunges into the distance
Horses no longer rise.
The two are troubled by the ravine;
Then the grass offers them a roof
That it built with a low branch.
Grief doesn't weep
Beneath the pink flowers of the heather.
Buzzards, kites, martens, ratters
And the dismal farandoles
Remain in the wilds.
The rye marks the frontier
Between the fern and the appeal.
To release an insignificant past.
What is needed,
With the bar of spring on the brow,
For the cloud to sleep
Without rolling at the edge of our eyes?
What is missing,
Joy of life and a stifled gallop,
An axe that's wedged between them?
Fight, sufferer! Get going, captive!
The sweat of the butchers
Still hypnotizes Mérindol.

Dans la plaie chimérique de Vaucluse je vous ai regardé souffrir. Là, bien qu'abaissé, vous étiez une eau verte, et encore une route. Vous traversiez la mort en son désordre. Fleur vallonnée d'un secret continu.

In the chimerical wound of Vaucluse I watched you suffer. There, though lowered, you were a green water and also a route. You were crossing death in its disarray. Undulated flower of an incessant secret.

L'ouragan dégarnit les bois.
J'endors, moi, la foudre aux yeux tendres.
Laissez le grand vent où je tremble
S'unir à la terre où je croîs.

Son souffle affile ma vigie.
Qu'il est trouble le creux du leurre
De la source aux couches salies!

Une clé sera ma demeure,
Feinte d'un feu que le coeur certifie;
Et l'air qui la tint dans ses serres.

The hurricane strips the woods. And I,
I lull to sleep the tender-eyed lightning.
Let the vast wind in which I tremble
Wed the earth in which I grow.

My vigil is sharpened by its breath.
How turbid the hollow of the lure
With its source of sullied beds.

A key will be my dwelling,
Feint of a fire certified by the heart;
And the air that clutched it in its claws.

Lorsque la douleur l'eut hissé sur son toit envié un savoir évident se montra à lui sans brouillard. Il ne se trouvait plus dans sa liberté telles deux rames au milieu de l'océan. L'ensorcelant désir de parole s'était, avec les eaux noires, retiré. Çà et là persistaient de menus tremblements dont il suivait le sillage aminci. Une colombe de granit à demi masquée mesurait de ses ailes les restes épars du grand oeuvre englouti. Sur les pentes humides, la queue des écumes et la course indigente des formes rompues. Dans l'ère rigoureuse qui s'ouvrait, aboli serait le privilège de récolter sans poison. Tous les ruisseaux libres et fous de la création avaient bien fini de ruer. Au terme de sa vie il devrait céder à l'audace nouvelle ce que l'immense patience lui avait, à chaque aurore, consenti. Le jour tournoyait sur Thouzon. La mort n'a pas comme le lichen arasé l'espérance de la neige. Dans le creux de la ville immergée, la corne de la lune mêlait le dernier sang et le premier limon.

When sorrow had hoisted him onto its coveted rooftop, a simple evidence, mistlessly, came clear. He was no longer free as two oars in the middle of the ocean. The spellbinding desire of speech had, along with the black waters, subsided. He followed the diminished wake of the slight tremblings that, here and there, still persisted. Half-masked, a granite dove measured with its wings the scattered remains of the great, engulfed work. Upon the damp slopes, the trail of foam and the indigent course of broken forms. In the stringent era that had just opened, the right to harvest without the use of poisons would be outlawed. The rush of all the free and raving streams of creation had completely ceased. At the end of his life he would have to yield to the new audacity everything that immense patience, with each dawn, had granted him. The day whirled about Thouzon. Unlike the lichen, death hasn't effaced all hope for snow. In the hollow of the immersed town, the moon's horn was mixing the last blood with the first clay.

Ils prennent pour de la clarté le rire jaune des ténèbres. Ils soupèsent dans leurs mains les restes de la mort et s'écrient: "Ce n'est pas pour nous." Aucun viatique précieux n'embellit la gueule de leurs serpents déroulés. Leur femme les trompe, leurs enfants les volent, leurs amis les raillent. Ils n'en distinguent rien, par haine de l'obscurité. Le diamant de la création jette-t-il des feux obliques? Promptement un leurre pour le couvrir. Ils ne poussent dans leur four, ils n'introduisent dans la pâte lisse de leur pain qu'une pincée de désespoir fromental. Ils se sont établis et prospèrent dans le berceau d'une mer où l'on s'est rendu maître des glaciers. Tu es prévenu.

Comment, faible écolier, convertir l'avenir et détiser ce feu tant questionné, tant remué, tombé sur ton regard fautif?

Le présent n'est qu'un jeu ou un massacre d'archers.

Dès lors fidèle à son amour comme le ciel l'est au rocher. Fidèle, méché, mais sans cesse vaguant, dérobant sa course par toute l'étendue montrée du feu, tenue du vent; l'étendue, trésor de boucher, sanglante à un croc.

They take for clarity the yellow laughter of the darkness. They weigh in their hands the remainders of death, and cry: "That's not for us." There's no precious viaticum to stud the mouth of their uncoiled snakes. Their wives deceive them, their children rob them, their friends ridicule them. Hating obscurity, they distinguish none of this. Does the diamond of creation glitter obliquely? Quickly, then, cover it with some enticement. They push into their ovens, they add into the smooth dough of their bread only a pinch of wheaten despair. While others have mastered the glaciers, they've settled and thrived within the cradle of the sea. You are forewarned.

How, frail schoolboy, will you convert the future and rake this fire, so questioned, so stirred, fallen onto your faulty watch?

The present is only a game or an archer's massacre.

Ever since, faithful to his love as the sky is to the rock. Faithful, fuse-bearing, but ceaselessly wandering, concealing his course throughout the entire expanse revealed by the fire and maintained by the wind; the expanse, the butcher's hoard, bleeding on a hook.

L'heureux temps. Chaque cité était une grande famille que la peur unissait; le chant des mains à l'oeuvre et la vivante nuit du ciel l'illuminaient. Le pollen de l'esprit gardait sa part d'exil.

Mais le présent perpétuel, le passé instantané, sous la fatigue maîtresse, ôtèrent les lisses.

Marche forcée, au terme épars. Enfants battus, chaume doré, hommes sanieux, tous à la roue! Visée par l'abeille de fer, la rose en larmes s'est ouverte.

A happy time! Each city was an enormous family unified by fear, lit by the song of hands at work and the sky's animated night. The pollen of the spirit kept its part of exile.

But the perpetual present, the instantaneous past, under the dominant fatigue, removed the handrails.

Forced march, with a scattered end. Whipped children, golden thatch, sanious men, all to the wheel! Aimed at by the iron bee, the rose in tears has opened.

J'ai reconnu dans un rocher la mort fuguée et mensurable, le lit ouvert de ses petits comparses sous la retraite d'un figuier. Nul signe de tailleur: chaque matin de la terre ouvrait ses ailes au bas des marches de la nuit.

Sans redite, allégé de la peur de hommes, je creuse dans l'air ma tombe et mon retour.

In a rock I recognized death, fugued and measurable, the open bed of its little accomplices beneath the shelter of a fig tree. Not a sign of a carver; at the base of night's stairway each morning of earth opened its wings.

Without repeating, freed of the fear of men, I dig in the air my tomb and my return.

Le passé retarderait l'éclosion du présent si nos souvenirs érodés n'y sommeillaient sans cesse. Nous nous retournons sur l'un tandis que l'autre marque un élan avant de se jeter sur nous.

De la ceinture de tisons au reposoir des morves. Du rêve gris au commerce avec rien. Course. Premier col: argile effritée.

La terre, est-ce quelque chose ou quelqu'un? Rien n'accourt lorsqu'appelle la question, sinon une large barre, un opaque anneau, et quelque serveuse d'approches.

Pour l'ère qui s'ouvre: "A la fin était le poison. Rien ne pouvait s'obtenir sans lui. Pas le moindre viatique humain. Pas la plus palpable récolte." Ainsi fulmine la terre glauque.

Contre l'épaisseur diffuse d'un somnambulisme empoisonné, la répugnance de l'esprit serait fuite chiffrée, serait, plus tard, révolte?

Jeunesse des dupes, girolle de la nuit.

Éteindre le tumulte, sans un porte-respect, comme se desserre à l'aube l'arc-en-ciel de la lune.

The past would delay the present's unfolding if our eroded memories hadn't slept there ceaselessly. We turn about on one while the other, before thrusting onto us, takes mark.

From the belt of fire-brands to the station of mucus. From a gray dream to an empty dealing. Course. First col: flaked clay.

Is the earth something or someone? Nothing rushes forth when the question calls except a wide bar, an opaque ring, and a waitress of approaches.

For the age that's beginning: "In the end was poison. Nothing could be obtained without it. Not the least human provision. Not the most palpable harvest." Thus the glaucous earth rages.

Against the extensive density of a poisoned somnambulism, would the spirit's disgust be coded escape; would it, later on, be revolt?

Youth of dupes, night's chanterelle.

Extinguish this turmoil, without a weapon, like the rainbow of the moon that loosens itself at dawn.

Nous ne jalousons pas les dieux, nous ne les servons pas, ne les craignons pas, mais au péril de notre vie nous attestons leur existence multiple, et nous nous émouvons d'être de leur élevage aventureux lorsque cesse leur souvenir.

Le vin de la liberté aigrit vite s'il n'est, à demi bu, rejeté au cep.

We are not jealous of the gods, we neither serve them nor fear them, but in peril of our lives we attest to their multiple existence, and are moved at belonging to their adventurous breed that no longer remembers them.

The wine of liberty quickly turns if, half-drunken, it isn't tossed back to the vine-stock.

Je t'ai montré La Petite-Pierre, la dot de sa forêt,
    le ciel qui naît aux branches,
L'ampleur de ses oiseaux chasseurs d'autres
    oiseaux,
Le pollen deux fois vivant sous la flambée des
    fleurs,
Une tour qu'on hisse au loin comme la toile du
    corsaire,
Le lac redevenu le berceau du moulin, le
    sommeil d'un enfant.

Là où m'oppressa ma ceinture de neige,
Sous l'auvent d'un rocher moucheté de corbeaux,
J'ai laissé le besoin d'hiver.
Nous nous aimons aujourd'hui sans au-delà et
    sans lignée,
Ardents ou effacés, différents mais ensemble,
Nous détournant des étoiles dont la nature est de
    voler sans parvenir.

Le navire fait route vers la haute mer végétale.
Tous feux éteints il nous prend à son bord.
Nous étions levés dès avant l'aube dans sa
    mémoire.
Il abrita nos enfances, lesta notre âge d'or,
L'appelé, l'hôte itinérant, tant que nous croyons
    à sa vérité.

I showed you La Petite-Pierre, the dowry of her
  forest, the sky that's born in her branches,
The richness of her birds, hunters of other birds,
The pollen twice alive beneath the blaze of
  flowers,
A tower hoisted far off like the sail of the
  corsair,
The lake that's once again the mill's cradle, the
  infant's sleep.

There, burdened by my belt of snow,
Beneath the visor of a rock speckled by crows,
I left the need of winter.
We love one another today without lineage and
  without what's beyond,
Ardent or unassuming, different but together,
Turning from the stars whose nature is to fly
  without arriving.

The ship makes its way toward the high vegetal
  sea.
All lights extinguished, it takes us aboard.
We were up before dawn in its memory.
It protected our childhood, ballasted our golden
  age.
This itinerant host, beckoned for as long as we
  believe in its truth.

En robe d'olivier

l'Amoureuse

avait dit:

Croyez à ma très enfantine fidélité.

Et depuis,

une vallée ouverte

une côte qui brille

un sentier d'alliance

ont envahi la ville

où la libre douleur est sous le vif de l'eau.

In the dress of an olive tree

the Lover

had said:

Trust in my very childish fidelity.

And since,

a sweeping valley

a glittering slope

a pathway of alliance

have assailed the city

where open sorrow is underneath the water's wash.

Les pierres se serrèrent dans le rempart et les hommes vécurent de la mousse des pierres. La pleine nuit portait fusil et les femmes n'accouchaient plus. L'ignominie avait l'aspet d'un verre d'eau.

Je me suis uni au courage de quelques êtres, j'ai vécu violemment, sans vieillir, mon mystère au milieu d'eux, j'ai frissonné de l'existence de tous les autres, comme une barque incontinente au-dessus des fonds cloisonnés.

The stones pressed against one another in the ramparts; off the moss of these stones men existed. Night carried a rifle and women would no longer give birth. Ignominy looked like a glass of water.

I am bound to the courage of several people; I've lived violently, without aging, my mystery among them. I have shuddered at the existence of all others like an incontinent boat about the segmented depths.

Cet homme n'était pas généreux parce qu'il voulait se voir généreux dans son miroir. Il était généreux parce qu'il venait des Pléiades et qu'il se détestait.

La même ombre prodigue, aux phalanges des doigts relevés, nous joignit lui et moi. Un soleil qui n'était point pour nous s'en échappa comme un père en faute ou mal gratifié.

This man wasn't generous because he wished to see himself so in his mirror. He was generous because he came from the Pleiades and hated himself.

The same profusive shadow with phalanges of uplifted fingers joined us together. A sun, meant for neither of us, vanished just like a guilty or ungratified father.

Qui l'entendit jamais se plaindre?

Nulle autre qu'elle n'aurait pu boire sans
   mourir les quarante fatigues,
Attendre, loin devant, ceux qui plieront après;
De l'éveil au couchant sa manoeuvre était
   mâle.

Qui a creusé le puits et hisse l'eau gisante
Risque son coeur dans l'écart de ses mains.

Whoever heard her complain?

No one but she could have drunken the forty
    hardships without dying,
Waiting far off for those who'll later succumb.
Her bearing, from dawn to dusk, was virile.

Whoever digs the well and raises the still water
Risks his heart in the spreading of his hands.

Porteront rameaux ceux dont l'endurance sait user la nuit noueuse qui précède et suit l'éclair. Leur parole reçoit existence du fruit intermittent qui la propage en se dilacérant. Ils sont les fils incestueux de l'entaille et du signe, qui élevèrent aux margelles le cercle en fleurs de la jarre du ralliement. La rage des vents les maintient encore dévêtus. Contre eux vole un duvet de nuit noire.

They'll bear branches, those whose endurance can exhaust the knotted night that precedes and follows the lightning. Their speech is instilled by the intermittent fruit and diffused by its splitting. They are the incestuous sons of the notch and sign that raised to the rims the flowering circle of the rallying jar. The winds' fury still keeps them unclothed. Against them a down of dark night flies.

En cette fin d'après-midi d'avril 1964 le vieil aigle despote, le maréchal-ferrant agenouillé, sous le nuage de feu de ses invectives (son travail, c'est-à-dire lui-même, il ne cessa de le fouetter d'offenses), me découvrit, à même le dallage de son atelier, la figure de Caroline, son modèle, le visage peint sur toile de Caroline—après combien de coups de griffes, de blessures, d'hématomes?—, fruit de passion entre tous les objets d'amour, victorieux du faux gigantisme des déchets additionnés de la mort, et aussi des parcelles lumineuses à peine séparées, de nous autres, ses témoins temporels. Hors de son alvéole de désir et de cruauté. Il se réfléchissait, ce beau visage sans antan qui allait tuer le sommeil, dans le miroir de notre regard, provisoire receveur universel pour tous les yeux futurs.

At this end of an afternoon in April 1964, the old despotic eagle, the kneeling blacksmith, under the flaming cloud of his abuses (endlessly thrashing his work, himself, that is, with insults) revealed to me, on the floor of his studio, the figure of Caroline, his model, Caroline's face on canvas—after how many scratches, wounds, bruises?—, fruit of passion above all of love's objects, triumphant over that mock enormity of the summed up scraps of death, and also over these luminous particles of ourselves, scarcely separated; ourselves, the temporal witnesses. Outside the canvas's alveole of desire and cruelty. This handsome face, without yesteryear, about to murder sleep, reflected in the mirror of our glance: the momentary, all-embracing recipient for every future eye.

—Je me suis promenée au bord de la Folie.—

Aux questions de mon coeur,
S'il ne les posait point,
Ma compagne cédait,
Tant est inventive l'absence.
Et ses yeux en décrue comme le Nil violet
Semblaient compter sans fin leurs gages
    s'allongeant
Dessous les pierres fraîches.

La Folie se coiffait de longs roseaux coupants.
Quelque part ce ruisseau vivait sa double vie.
L'or cruel de son nom soudain envahisseur
Venait livrer bataille à la fortune adverse.

—I walked along the edge of the Folie.—

To the unmentioned questions of my heart
My companion yielded,
So inventive is absence.
And her eyes in ebbing, a violet Nile,
Seemed to be ceaselessly counting their tokens,
    spread
Out underneath the fresh stones.

The Folie dressed itself with long tapering
    weeds.
Somewhere this stream lived its double life.
Suddenly invading, the bitter gold of its name
Advanced into battle against adverse fortune.

Tant il gela que les branches laiteuses
Molestèrent la scie, se cassèrent aux mains.
Le printemps ne vit pas verdir les gracieuses.

Le figuier demanda au maître du gisant
L'arbuste d'une foi nouvelle.
Mais le loriot, son prophète,
L'aube chaude de son retour,
En se posant sure le désastre,
Au lieu de faim, périt d'amour.

So much it froze that the milky branches
Hurt the saw, and snapped in the hands.
Spring didn't see the gracious ones turn green.

From the master of the felled, the fig tree
Asked for the shrub of a new faith.
But the oriole, its prophet,
The warm dawn of his return,
Alighting upon the disaster,
Instead of hunger, died of love.

La reculée aux sources: devant les arbustes épineux, sur un couloir d'air frais, un blâme-barrière arrête l'assoiffé. Les eaux des mécénats printainiers et l'empreinte du visage provident vaguent, distantes, par l'impraticable delta.

Revers des sources: pays d'amont, pays sans biens, hôte pelé, je roule ma chance vers vous. M'étant trop peu soucié d'elle, elle irriguait, besogne plane, le jardin de vos ennemis. La faute est levée.

Retreat to the sources: beyond the spiky bushes, in a channel of fresh air, the thirsting are stopped by a blaming-gate. Waters of vernal benefaction, tracings of the provident face, each roam distantly upon the unfeasible delta.

Reverse of the sources: the regions upland, land without assets, ravished host, towards you I'm casting my lot. In my carelessness, it irrigated—a level task—the garden of your enemies. The fault is lifted.

Tels des loups ennoblis
Par leur disparition,
Nous guettons l'an de crainte
Et de libération.

Les loups enneigés
Des lointaines battues,
A la date effacée.

Sous l'avenir qui gronde,
Furtifs, nous attendons,
Pour nous affilier,
L'amplitude d'amont.

Nous savons que les Choses arrivent
Soudainement,
Sombres ou trop ornées.

Le dard qui liait les deux draps
Vie contre vie, clameur et mont,
Fulgura.

Such as wolves, so ennobled
Since their disappearance,
We're watching for the year
Of dread, and deliverance.

The wolves, snow-glazed,
In the distant trackings,
At a time, now effaced.

Under the future's rumble,
Furtives, we wait,
To band with one another, the
Amplitude upland.

We are aware that Things arrive
Suddenly,
Somber or too ornate.

The dart binding two sheets,
Life to life, clamor and mount,
Flashed.

Joue contre joue deux gueuses en leur détresse
    roidie;
La gelée et le vent ne les ont point instruites,
    les ont négligées;
Enfants d'arrière-histoire
Tombées des saisons dépassantes et serrées là
    debout.
Nulles lèvres pour les transposer, l'heure
    tourne.
Il n'y aura ni rapt, ni rancune.
Et qui marche passe sans regard devant elles,
    devant nous.
Deux roses perforées d'un anneau profond
Mettent dans leur étrangeté un peu de défi.
Perd-on la vie autrement que par les épines?
Mais par la fleur, les longs jours l'ont su!
Et le soleil a cessé d'être initial.
Une nuit, le jour bas, tout le risque, deux roses,
Comme la flamme sous l'abri, joue contre joue
    avec qui la tue.

Cheek to cheek, two beggars in stiffened
    distress,
Untrained by the wind and frost, and
    unheeded;
Children of an aforetime
Fallen from extended seasons, that stand there,
Huddled. Without lips to transpose them the
    hours turn.
There won't be abduction or avenging, and
No one that passes notices them, notices us.
Two roses, drilled with a deep-set ring,
Add to their oddity a touch of defiance.
Can anything, aside from the thorns, bring an
    end to life?
As the long days always knew: the flower!
And the sun is no longer initiate.
One night, the lowered day, the entire risk,
    two roses,
Like the flame within its shelter, cheek to
    cheek with what kills it.

Il faut escalader beaucoup de dogmes et de glace pour jouer de bonheur et s'éveiller rougeur sur la pierre du lit.

Entre eux et moi il y eut longtemps comme une haie sauvage dont il nous était loisible de recueillir les aubépines en fleurs, et de nous les offrir. Jamais plus loin que la main et le bras. Ils m'aimaient et je les aimais. Cet obstacle *pour le vent* où échouait ma pleine force, quel était-il? Un rossignol me le révéla, et puis une charogne.

La mort dans la vie, c'est inalliable, c'est répugnant; la mort avec la mort, c'est approchable, ce n'est rien, un ventre peureux y rampe sans trembler.

J'ai renversé le dernier mur, celui qui ceinture les nomades des neiges, et je vois—ô mes premiers parents—l'été du chandelier.

Notre figure terrestre n'est que le second tiers d'une poursuite continue, un point, amont.

One has to scale so much ice and dogma before attaining pleasure and awaking—flushed—on the stone of the bed.

For some time there'd been, between them and me, something like a wild hedge. We were free to pick and offer one another its flowering hawthorne. But never further than a hand's, an arm's length. They loved me just as I loved them. What was it, though, that obstacle *to the wind* in which my full strength failed? It was a nightingale that first revealed it to me, then carrion.

Death in life is repugnant, nonalloyable; death, however, within death is something accessible, is nothing: a frightened belly could crawl there without trembling.

I have overthrown the last wall, the one that encircles the snow nomads, and I see—o my very first parents—the candelabra's summer.

Our figure on earth is only the second third of a continuous pursuit, a point, upland.

Par une terre d'Ombre et de rampes sanguines nous retournions aux rues. Le timon de l'amour ne nous dépassait pas, ne gagnait plus sur nous. Tu ouvris ta main et m'en montras les lignes. Mais la nuit s'y haussait. Je déposai l'infime ver luisant sur le tracé de vie. Des années de gisant s'éclairèrent soudain sous ce fanal vivant et altéré de nous.

We returned to the streets through sanguine slopes and an Umbrian land. The helm of love wasn't passing us, and now no longer gained. You opened your hand and showed me its lines. But there the night rose. Onto the tracing of life I placed the feeble glow-worm. Beneath this lamp, alive and athirst for us, years and years of recumbency suddenly lit.

Tu étais folle.

Comme c'est loin!

Tu mourus, un doigt devant ta bouche,
Dans un noble mouvement,
Pour couper court à l'effusion;
Au froid soleil d'un vert partage.

Tu étais si belle que nul ne s'aperçut de ta
    mort.
Plus tard, c'était la nuit, tu te mis en chemin
    avec moi.

Nudité sans méfiance,
Seins pourris par ton coeur.

A l'aise en ce monde occurrent,
Un homme, qui t'avait serrée dans ses bras,
Passa à table.

Sois bien, tu n'es pas.

You were mad.

O, that was so long ago!

You died, a finger in front of your mouth,
In an elegant gesture
That checked effusion
In the freezing sun of a green partition.

You were so lovely no one even noticed your
    death.
Later, it was night; you set out alongside me.

Unsuspecting nudity,
Breasts corrupted by your heart.

Comfortable in this occuring world,
A man who'd held you in his arms
Took his place at table.

Be well. You don't exist.

SERVANTE

Tu es une fois encore la bougie où sombrent les
ténèbres autour d'un nouvel insurgé, Toi sur qui se
lève un fouet qui s'emporte à ta clarté qui pleure.

SERVANT

You are once again the candle where the darkness sinks around a new insurgent; against You a whip rises, infuriated by your clarity that cries.

Dans le ciel des hommes, le pain des étoiles me sembla ténébreux et durci, mais dans leurs mains étroites je lus la joute de ces étoiles en invitant d'autres: émigrantes du pont encore rêveuses; j'en recueillis la sueur dorée, et par moi la terre cessa de mourir.

The bread of the stars seemed to me, in the sky of men, dark and hardened; but in their narrow hands, I read the joust of these stars, inviting others: the still musing emigrants of the deck. I garnered their golden sweat and, through me, the earth no longer died.

La nuit était ancienne
Quand le feu l'entrouvrit.
Ainsi de ma maison.

On ne tue point la rose
Dans les guerres du ciel.
On exile une lyre.

Mon chagrin persistant,
D'un nuage de neige
Obtient un lac de sang.
Cruauté aime vivre.

O source qui mentis
A nos destins jumeaux,
J'élèverai du loup
Ce seul portrait pensif!

Night was ancient
When the fire wedged through.
So it was with my house.

A rose isn't slaughtered
In the wars of the sky.
But a lyre is banished.

From a cloud of snow
My persisting sorrow
Obtains a lake of blood.
Cruelty loves to live.

O source that lied
To our twin destinies,
I will raise up from the wolf
This single, pensive portrait.

Oreiller rouge, oreiller noir,
Sommeil, un sein sur le côté,
Entre l'étoile et le carré,
Que de bannières en débris!

Trancher, en finir avec vous,
Comme le moût est à la cuve,
Dans l'espoir de lèvres dorées.

Moyeu de l'air fondamental
Durcissant l'eau des blancs marais,
Sans souffrir, enfin sans souffrance,
Admis dans le verbe frileux,
Je dirai: "Monte" au cercle chaud.

Red pillow and black pillow,
Sleep, a breast on its side,
Between the star and square
So many pennants in tatters!

Foreshorten, to end with you,
As the must, arrived in its vat,
With the hope, lips of gold.

Hub of the fundamental air,
Hardening the water of white marshes,
Without suffering, at least without suffrance,
Admitted into the chilly verb,
I'll say "climb" to the warm circle.

Affermi par la bonté d'un fruit hivernal, je rentrai le feu dans la maison. La civilisation des orages gouttait à la génoise du toit. Je pourrai à loisir haïr la tradition, rêver au givre des passants sur des sentiers peu vétilleux. Mais confier à qui mes enfants jamais nés? La solitude était privée de ses épices, la flamme blanche s'enlisait, n'offrant de sa chaleur que le geste expirant.

Sans solennité je franchis ce monde muré: j'aimerai sans manteau ce qui tremblait sous moi.

Strengthened by the goodness of a winter fruit, I brought the fire into the house. The civilization of storms dripped from the overhanging tiles. I'll now be free to detest tradition, to dream of the frost of those that passed on the scarcely captious pathways. But to whom will I entrust my unborn children? Solitude was without its spaces; the white flame sank and its warmth only offered an expiring gesture.

Without solemnity I leapt over this walled-in world; coatless, I'll love whatever trembled beneath me.

On ne se console de rien lorsqu'on marche en tenant une main, la périlleuse floraison de la chair d'une main.

L'obscurcissement de la main qui nous presse et nous entraîne, innocente aussi, l'odorante main où nous nous ajoutons et gardons ressource, ne nous évitant pas le ravin et l'épine, le feu prématuré, l'encerclement des hommes, cette main préférée à toutes, nous enlève à la duplication de l'ombre, au jour du soir. Au jour brillant au-dessus du soir, froissé son seuil d'agonie.

There is nothing to console us when we walk, holding a hand, the perilous blossoming of the flesh of a hand.

The obscuring of the hand, pressing and pulling us, this innocent, this fragrant hand into which we add ourselves and subsist, that spares us neither thorns nor ravines, neither the premature fire nor the encirclement of men, this hand, the most beloved of all, removes us from the shadow's duplication at the daylight of evening. The daylight, glittering above evening, when its threshold of agony has crumpled.

L'ouest derrière soi perdu, présumé englouti, touché de rien, hors-mémoire, s'arrache à sa couche elliptique, monte sans s'essouffler, enfin se hisse et rejoint. Le point fond. Les sources versent. Amont éclate. Et en bas le delta verdit. Le chant des frontières s'étend jusqu'au belvédère d'aval. Content de peu est le pollen des aulnes.

The west vanished behind us, seemingly swallowed, touched by nothing and beyond all memory, tears itself from its elliptic couch, climbs in keeping its breath, and finally rises and rejoins. The point melts. The sources gush. Upland bursts. And below, the delta turns green. The song of the frontiers spreads to within sight of the lowlands. Pleased with so little is the pollen of the alder.

Appendix: Variant Translations

THE POPLAR'S EFFACEMENT

The hurricane strips bare the woods.
And I, I lull to sleep the tender-eyed lightning.
Let the high wind I tremble in
Bind itself to the earth in which I grow.

Its breath sharpens my vigil.
How turbid the hollow of the lure
From the source to the sullied beds.

A key will become my dwelling,
Feint of a fire vouched for by the heart,
And the air that clutched it in its claws.

CHERISHING THOUZON

When sorrow had hoisted him onto its coveted roof,
an unmistakable knowledge mistlessly revealed itself.
He was no longer set in his liberty as two oars in the
middle of the ocean. The spellbinding desire for speech,

Translations in this section are found in Gustaf Sobin's papers but
there is no clear indication they were considered less final than
those included in the main text above. There are, however, reasons
to assign them to an earlier period.

along with the black waters, had subsided. He followed the diminished wake of the slight tremblings that, here and there, still persisted. Half-masked, a granite dove measured with its wings the scattered remains of the great work, engulfed. On the damp slopes, the trail of foam and the indigent course of broken forms. In the stringent era, just beginning, the right to harvest without poison would be abolished. The kick of all the free and raving streams of creation had completely ceased. At the end of his life he would have to yield to the new audacity everything immense patience, with each dawn, had granted him. The day whirled around Thouzon. Unlike the razed lichen, death cannot hope for snow. In the hollow of the immersed town the moon's horn mixed the last blood with the first clay.

MIRAGE OF THE NEEDLES

They take for clarity the yellow laughter of the darkness. They weigh in their hands the remnants of death, and cry out: "that's not for us." No precious viaticum studs the jaw of their uncoiled snakes. They're deceived by their wives, robbed by their children, mocked at by their friends. Loathing obscurity, they notice nothing. Does the diamond of creation glitter obliquely? Quickly, then, cover it with some distraction. They push into their ovens, they add to the smooth dough of their bread only a pinch of wheaten despair. They've settled and thrived within the cradle of a sea where others have mastered the glaciers. You are forewarned.

How, frail schoolboy, convert the future and rake

out this fire that, so questioned, so stirred, has fallen onto your faulty gaze?

The present is only a game or a massacre of archers.

Ever since, faithful to his love as the sky is to the rock. Faithful, fuse-bearing, but ceaselessly vagrant, concealing his course throughout the entire expanse revealed by the fire and maintained by the wind: the expanse, the butcher's hoard, that bleeds from its hook.

AT THE GATEWAYS OF AEREA

It was a happy time. Each city was an enormous family bound together by fear and lit by the song of hands at work and the living night of the sky. As for the pollen of the spirit, it safeguarded its part of exile.

But the perpetual present, the instantaneous past, under the dominant exhaustion, removed the handrails.

Forced march to a scattered end. Whipped children, golden thatch, sanious men, all to the wheel! Sighted by the iron bee, the rose in tears has broken open.

CELEBRATING GIACOMETTI

At this end of an afternoon in April 1964, the old despotic eagle, the kneeling blacksmith under the flaming cloud of his curses (thrashing his work—himself, that is— with endless insults) showed me, on the very floor of his studio, the figure of Caroline, his model, Caroline's face on canvas—after how many scratches, wounds, bruises?— the fruit of passion above all love's objects, triumphant over that mock enormity of death's swept-up scraps; over, too, those luminous, scarcely separated particles, ours, the itinerant witnesses. Outside that cell of cruelty and desire. This handsome face, without a past and on its way to murder sleep, reflected in the mirror of our gaze, the momentary, all-embracing recipient for every future eye.

SEPTENTRION

—I walked along the edge of the Folie.—

To the questions of my heart,
If none were forthcoming,
My companion yielded,
So inventive is absence.
And her eyes at ebb like the violet Nile
Seemed to be endlessly counting their tokens
Spread out underneath the fresh stones.

The Folie dressed itself with long, tapering reeds.
Somewhere this stream lived its double life.
Suddenly invasive, the cruel gold of its name
Came to wage battle against adverse fortune.

LYRIC OF THE FIG TREE

So much it froze that the milky branches
Harmed the saw and snapped in the hands.
Spring didn't see the gracious ones green.

The fig tree asked the master of the recumbent
For the shrub of a new faith.
But the oriole, his prophet,

The warm dawn of his return,
Alighting upon the disaster,
Instead of hunger, died of love.

OCTOBER'S JUDGMENT

Cheek to cheek, two vagabonds, stiff in their
    distress,
Schooled by neither wind nor frost, and unheeded;
Children of another time,
Fallen from spent seasons and huddled there, on
    end.
Without lips to transpose them, the hours turn.
They won't be either cursed or coveted, and
Whoever passes will pass without noticing them,
    without noticing us.
Two roses, drilled with a deep-set ring
Add to their oddity a touch of defiance.
Can anything, aside from the thorns, put an end to
    life?
As the long days always knew: the flower!
And the sun has ceased to initiate.
One night, the day low, the entire risk, two roses
Like the flame within its shelter, cheek to cheek
    with whatever kills it.

SLOWNESS OF THE FUTURE

We must scale so much ice and dogma before
running into good fortune, before waking in redness on
the stone of the bed.

For a long while there had been, between them and me, something like a wild hedge; we were free to pick and offer one another its flowering hawthorne. Never further than the hand and the arm. They loved me just as I loved them. But what was this obstacle *to the wind* where my full strength failed? It was revealed to me by a nightingale and then, by carrion.

Death within life is repugnant, irreconcilable; death with death, though, is approachable, it's nothing: a frightened belly can crawl there without quivering.

I have overthrown the last wall, the one that encircles the snow nomads, and I see—o my very first parents—the candlestick's summer.

Our figure on earth is only the second third of an incessant pursuit, a point, upland.

SERVANT

You are once again the candle where the darkness settles about a new insurgent, You against whom a whip rises, infuriated by your clarity that weeps.

A Glossary of Place Names

Aerea: A town in Gaul within the region now named the Vaucluse, mentioned by Pliny the Younger and Strabo. It has totally disappeared and its exact placement is disputed.

Baronnies: Buis-les-Baronnies, a town just north of the Vaucluse, surrounded by hills terraced with olive orchards.

Buoux: A small community along the northern slopes of the Luberon. Above it are the boat-shaped ruins of a Vaudois fortress and, far off, the tower of a priory.

La Brémonde: A fruit and grain farm in the region of Buoux.

La Folie: A small stream in the Vaucluse named after its unpredictable current.

La Petite-Pierre: A town and its surrounding forests in Alsace.

Luberon: A long range of pre-Alpine mountains in Provence.

_____

Compiled by Gustaf Sobin.

Merindol: A Village on the southern slopes of the Luberon, devastated by plague, the War of Religions and by the Nazi occupation.

Thouzon: A castle and monastery, ruined in the Middle Ages, lying on a hill overlooking the town of Le Thor, Vaucluse.

Vaucluse: Fontaine de Vaucluse, the town and cavernous source of the river Sorgue. Since the Romans it has given its name to the entire region (or departement).

Venasque: A perched village on the Plateau de Vaucluse.

About the Author

René Char (1907–1988) was one of the most important modern French poets. Admired by Heidegger for his poetic philosophy, he was a hero of the French Resistance and in the 1960s a militant anti-nuclear protester. Associated with the Surrealist movement for several years and a close friend of many painters—notably Braque, Giacometti, and Picasso—he wrote poetry that confronted major twentieth century moral, political, and artistic concerns.

About the Translator

Gustaf Sobin (1935–2005) was born in Boston but lived most of his life in the Provence region of France. Among his many books are *Breath's Burials* (poetry, New Directions, 1995), *Luminous Debris* (1999) and *Ladder of Shadows* (2008) (essays, University of California Press), *Aura: Last Essays* (Counterpath Press, 2008), and *Collected Poems* (Talisman House, forthcoming).